Befriending the Prophets

Howard R. Macy

BARCLAY PRESS
Newberg, OR 97132

Befriending the Prophets

©2023 by Howard R. Macy

Barclay Press, Inc.
Newberg, Oregon
www.barclaypress.com

All rights reserved. No part may be reproduced
for any commercial purpose by any method without
permission in writing from the copyright holder.

Printed in the United States of America

Cover and page design by Mareesa Fawver Moss

Cover photo by Johann Siemens

ISBN 978-1-59498-106-7

My chief objection to prophets is our tendency to ignore them until they're dead. In this wonderful book, Howard Macy helps us see what we too often miss—that God raises up prophets to teach us when to say "Yes," when to say "No," and to whom. If you're looking for an accessible primer on the prophetic life and role, you've found it.

Phil Gulley
author of *If the Church Were Christian*

Befriending the Prophets deftly unveils much of the mystery surrounding the biblical prophets but without minimizing their legitimacy and authenticity. By paying attention to call, vision, values and listening, Howard Macy establishes key points that ground the prophetic commitment in the service of God. In the process, he makes a convincing case that there is still prophetic work to be done, perhaps even by the likes of you and me.

Jay Marshall
Dean Emeritus, Earlham School of Religion, and
author of *When the Spirit Calls*

I cannot recall the last time I preached on the biblical prophets, but that is going to change. Howard Macy has reintroduced his readers to these neglected characters and revived their messages for our times. More than ever, we need "disturbing people" willing to guide and challenge us in the ways of righteousness, justice, love, and truth. Throughout this book, you will find a renewed call to pick up this prophetic mantle and bring peace and hope to our world.

Dr. Robert S. Henry
pastor at Indianapolis First
Friends Quaker Meeting

Learning about the Hebrew prophets from Howard, when I was his student at Friends University, transformed my understanding of them. His ability to make these figures relatable caught me then, even as *Befriending the Prophets* does now. With imagination, wisdom, and wit, Howard shows us why their message is as relevant and timely as ever.

Buy this book and share it widely!

Kendra Weddle, Ph.D.
Scholar-in-Residence,
Northaven Church, Dallas, Texas

As a professor of Old Testament, I am grateful for Howard Macy's life and scholarship that contributes to such an accessible, inspiring, informative, and rich resource on the prophets. Macy invites the reader on an integrative experience of the prophetic role, drawing us in to see the prophets as experienced and faithful listeners, captured by God's compelling vision of life together, as a community that seeks peace (*shalom*). Highly recommended!

Jennifer M. Matheny

(Ph.D. University of Kent, UK) recently named an associate professor of Christian Scriptures at Baylor University's George W. Truett Theological Seminary. Recent and forthcoming books include *Judges 19-21 and Ruth: Canon as a Voice of Answerability* (Brill, August 2022) and *Hesed and the Core of Old Testament Theology* (Baker Academic, forthcoming August 2024).

Befriending the Prophets is warm, engaging, delightful and disturbing. To be sure, it challenges many of our most cherished misconceptions of the Hebrew prophets. Most helpful of all, it provides us with a wise understanding of the role of the prophet in our day. I highly recommend *Befriending the Prophets* to you for your reading, studying, reflecting, and praying.

Richard J. Foster

author of several books including
Celebration of Discipline and *Learning Humility*

In his serious yet playful invitation to befriend the prophets, Howard Macy invites us into a more profound and more transformational journey than simply sharpening our understanding of a unique form of biblical literature. Instead, as we learn to know and love those who dared speak for God, we come face to face with the God who speaks and acts in human history. *Befriending the Prophets* reminds us that God proclaims and demonstrates peace, justice, righteousness, and overwhelming mercy through those willing to listen and obey—both long ago and today.

Colin Saxton
Quaker minister and co-author of
Walking with the Bible (Pendle Hill, 2022)

In this winsome book, Howard Macy invites us to come alongside Israel's prophets, gaining a sense of what Abraham Heschel described as the *pathos* of God for humanity. Were they saints, cranks, or something in between? With his insightful treatments of these key biblical figures and their messages, Howard helps them become our life-changing friends.

Paul N. Anderson
author of *Following Jesus:*
The Heart of Faith and Practice

For friend
David Wetherell
in memory and gratitude

Contents

11 Introduction
17 Getting Acquainted
31 Captured by God
41 Compelling Vision
53 Experienced Listeners
65 Beyond Cranky
75 Scripture Index

Introduction

The several churches in which I grew up largely neglected the biblical prophets except for some folks who liked to speculate about when the world might end. (The answer was always "soon.") Though these congregations valued the Bible, they did not regularly include the prophets as part of teaching or of the public reading of Scripture. So I didn't learn much about who the prophets were, what they did, or what they had to say. This is a common story, and, for a variety of reasons, many others know little about the prophets.

Happily, over the years I have learned more and have come to cherish the prophets. Both who they were and what they said guide me in living faithfully. Through my teaching in the church and in college classrooms, I have also learned some of the questions, barriers, and misleading ideas that hinder people from coming to know the prophets for themselves. I hope that this series of essays can overcome some of those hindrances and can invite readers to join me in befriending the prophets.

These essays will focus on the prophets as a group—more like taking a family photo than creating individual portraits. Most of the family photos I've seen work pretty well, though they often include an eccentric uncle or some goofy cousins. Together they still give you the picture. The essays will leave loose ends, unanswered questions. I haven't tried to write a textbook, neither in scope nor in technical language. So again, I invite you in.

Some readers may wander easily through the prophets and the Hebrew Scriptures without fear. However, I'm sure that many others would wander and might well get lost. So, as a help to any who would like it, I'm including below a short introduction or refresher essay that will help give an overview of the territory.

***

A common short description says, "The prophets spoke to the people for God and to God for the people." Its simplicity captures the basics. Another common way of speaking of the prophets is to note that, in Israel, there were three offices: prophet, priest, and king. This honors the reality that the prophets played a significant role, though it neglects the fact that it isn't an official role, unlike those of the royal and priestly families. Prophets were appointed only by God.

Of the several metaphors people use to speak of the role of the prophet, I find the idea of "ambassador" compelling. An ambassador represents a particular government and is authorized to speak on behalf of that government. In a sense, prophets are ambassadors of God's government, God's realm, which is much broader than simply the people of Israel and their kingdoms of Israel and Judah. The Israelites understood that God's sovereignty extends over all the earth, over all of creation. So the prophets come as ambassadors from that realm, speaking with the authority of that sovereign. For the prophets, being in between God and the people they belonged to and loved was often awkward and sometimes painful, particularly if the message they had to deliver was harsh.

Most of the prophets we know about lived during the years of Israel's monarchy and a bit beyond, roughly 1000–400 BCE, beginning with the prophet Samuel. (More detailed introductions than mine would explain why "roughly" is used to describe the dates mentioned.) The Bible mentions several prophets before that time, for example, Abraham (for praying on behalf of King Abimelech); Moses and Miriam; and Deborah (both a judge and a prophet).

Samuel appears first in the period often referred to as the Early Prophets, from about 1000–800 BCE. We have stories from this time about the prophets Nathan, Elijah, and Elisha, though we have stories of others who are named and of some who are not. Typically the stories tell us the occasion of a prophet's speech or action, what the prophet said or did, and the outcome. We find these accounts in what Christians call the historical books: Samuel, Kings, and Chronicles. In the Hebrew Scriptures, these historical books are called the Former Prophets, which points to the prominence of prophets throughout their pages.

In contrast, what Christian Bibles group as the Prophets (or, more casually, the writing prophets), the Hebrew Scriptures call the Latter Prophets. These books collect the oracles and actions of prophets from after 800 BCE and beyond, including Amos, Hosea, Isaiah, Jeremiah, Ezekiel, and several others. Typically we find less narrative about the prophets and collections of longer or shorter speeches, often without clear context or divisions. (The editors and translators of modern Bibles often suggest divisions and section titles to help readers.) The early prophets come to us in books that include historical writing about kings, dynasties, international conflicts, and more. The latter prophets come to us in books that are devoted to the ministry of individual prophets, though still clearly in a historical context.

For the purposes of our family photo of prophets here, we will treat the prophets as very much alike over the centuries. They share similarities in their interactions with kings and queens, their messages to the people, their calls, and their common themes.

The Christian Scriptures also include prophets. The Gospels note, of course, John the Baptist and Jesus. In the life of the early church, we see persons who are identified as prophets, and we see the practice and gift of prophecy. We'll say more about that in the essays.

Getting Acquainted

Maybe you've already survived the end of the world several times. Maybe you think we are living in the end of the world. Maybe you're sure you have the prophets figured out. Maybe the prophets puzzle you. Wherever you are, I want to invite you to become companions to the Hebrew prophets, a group that Abraham Joshua Heschel called "some of the most disturbing people who have ever lived."[1] I will urge you to befriend them, to come alongside them, and to risk becoming a disturbing person yourself.

---

1. Abraham Heschel, *The Prophets* (New York: Harper and Row, 1962), I, ix.

The world needs more disturbing people—people who can envision the wonders of life together that God intends for us, people who can see through and call out the ways we corrupt that life, people who can teach us how to walk in God's ways. The prophets were people like that. As we befriend them, we can learn from them. We might even be drawn to become like them.

You probably can name some of the obstacles to befriending the prophets. Often people misunderstand the role and character of the prophets. Many modern folk struggle just to read the prophets for a variety of sensible reasons. Others hold misleading expectations about what they can learn from the prophets, often missing what they have to say while looking for things they don't. Sometimes people will set prophets apart as characters we should admire but who aren't well connected to ordinary life. The prophets can be weird. Granted. But they're not a lot weirder, let's give ourselves a little credit here, than you and I.

People often think of prophets in ways that block knowing who they were (and are). The prophets, they're convinced, are cranks or eccentrics or social activists or purveyors of vague clues about the end of the world. But the prophets' role was more rounded than that. Let me offer a definition I work with: a prophet is a visible sign and enduring witness that God is here, that God cares, and that God is actively working to renew wholeness (*shalom*) in all creation. I like Eugene Peterson's brief definition, too: "A prophet is a person who sees what God is doing and then tells us so we can get in on it."[2]

The Hebrew prophets were present to the Israelites in particular times and places to offer guidance, to correct, to warn, to offer hope, and to speak and act as the moment required. In the Hebrew Scriptures we have a record of what they did, sometimes in story, but more often in collections of sayings.

One of the obstacles to befriending the prophets is that reading from them is difficult, for sensible reasons. Sometimes it's simply a problem of unfriendly translations. Just as a practical matter, the King James Version was authorized more than four hundred years ago, and the English language has changed enormously in form and vocabulary since then. And

---

2. Eugene H. Peterson, *As Kingfishers Catch Fire* (New York: Waterbrook, 2017), 131.

traditional typesetting and page design can obscure the forms of the text. The traditional translation has wonderful phrases that many of us still cherish, but in many ways, it blocks our access to the meaning of the texts. Reliable modern editions, several of which are widely regarded, offer more precise translations and use page design that helps readers see the poetic character of texts and where sections begin and end. In general, I encourage people to read translations that use an English that sounds like them. (There are limits here, of course.)

Another obstacle in reading is that these accounts and sayings of the prophets originate in specific times and places, in ancient Israel roughly 2,500 years ago. So they will refer to names, places, and events that, without some background, we won't recognize, and they will use themes associated with people and places that we don't understand. When we impose our modern cultural understandings on ancient texts, we often miss the point or distort it. Maybe this seems too obvious, but my experience in teaching and in the life of the church suggests that I shouldn't ignore it. In fact, sometimes interpreters get into trouble for making such an obvious point.

To help overcome these gaps in history and cultures, I suggest that readers use a good study Bible that includes notes to explain names, places, and key ideas but that isn't weaving all of these into an elaborate interpretive scheme. Over the years, I have found several study Bibles that offer excellent help.

Another sensible obstacle in reading is that most of the content in the books of the prophets is written in poetry. And you have to read poetry differently than prose. The form is different, the poetic lines tend to be compact, and it often uses vivid, sometimes jarring, language. Generally you can't speed-read poetry, though that sort of rushed, controlling reading is how we tend to read almost everything (like a quick scan of the newspaper obituaries to make sure you're not there). Instead, with poetry, you have to listen patiently, soak in it, let it soak into you. Let the images live and the word plays do their job. Slow down and listen. Sometimes it even helps to read aloud thoughtfully, not just rattling through.

Misleading expectations about what the prophets are doing also hinder catching on to the prophets. Here again, we must speak of time and place. God sent prophets to particular people in specific circumstances to give them words of guidance and hope, of warning and correction. And we should expect that those people could understand and respond to what they were told. We should not expect that the prophets' messages seemed coded and baffling to their contemporaries and would only make sense to smart folks who lived many centuries later, like now. Certainly many of their messages and themes endure and teach us still. "Act justly, love mercy, walk humbly with God" (Micah 6:8). "I desire steadfast love and not sacrifice" (Hosea 6:6). "Let justice roll down like waters, and righteousness like an ever-flowing stream" (Amos 5:24). Such great themes still challenge and stretch us, though prophetic guidance to surrender to Babylon will make less sense today.

Misleadingly, however, many folks scour the prophets, looking for secret clues buried there to tell us about our century and even to let us calculate the end of the world as we know it. As an older guy, please know that I'm not hardened or cynical by the fact that I've missed the end of the world several times (1988 may be my favorite), perhaps even more times than I know since I surely missed some of the dated predictions.

Instead, I am quite sure God is more invested in calling people to treat others fairly; to show love to neighbors and strangers; to help out the poor, needy, and vulnerable; and to collaborate in God's peaceable kingdom purposes in the world. God did not seed prophetic messages with obscure clues for professional prognosticators to tease out 2,000 years later.

Of course, the prophets made predictions, though these are only part of what the prophets had to say. And often predictions offer warnings more than fixed events. The prophets hoped the people would change their ways and avoid disaster. Sometimes the people listened and changed. Rather than warnings, however, some predictions brought words of hope promising rescue or restoration. And the Bible reports how these promises were fulfilled.

Trying to tease out hidden meanings, mostly to serve our curiosity and need to control, generally obscures what the prophets have to say. Too easily we can miss what the prophets have to say while we're looking for things they don't say. The clear witness and major themes of the prophets, if we receive them, will challenge us to live well today as fully as they did the original hearers.

Still another obstacle in befriending the prophets is how often we push them away as being unapproachable. We commonly distance ourselves from remarkably faithful people by calling them a saint, a mystic, or a prophet, and in doing so, we dismiss the idea that we could be like them. It makes them superhuman, not even remotely like us. This is misleading.

I grew up in a religious culture that discouraged calling people saints, perhaps in reaction to Christian traditions full of saint's days and saints for this and that. But I think differently about that now. Partly that comes from learning that the Apostle Paul (Saint Paul?) didn't hesitate to call people saints and partly from knowing that the folks who have come to be recognized as saints were ordinary persons in whom people saw remarkable service and devotion to God. None of them, as nearly as I know, set out to earn a saint badge to put on their uniform. In fact, I'm sure most of them would be surprised, even embarrassed, to be called a saint. All they did was to live in steady faithfulness day to day, doing what seemed necessary—feeding the poor, helping the needy, bringing healing, boldly telling the truth, being present in sharing the love of God. For me, learning about the saints reminds me of how faithfully all of us can actually live ordinary life a day at a time.

Similarly, people often use the word "mystic" to set a person apart as odd and very unlike themselves. Evelyn Underhill, a scholar of mysticism with all the complexities people bring to that word, tries to keep it simple: "A mystic is not a person who has queer experiences; but a person for whom God is the one reality of life, the supreme Object of love. . . . A mystic is not a person who practises unusual forms of prayer, but a person whose life is ruled by this thirst [for God]."[3] This thirst for God belongs, at least potentially, to all of us, and the mystics are people who follow it, whose lives are shaped by it. I'm sure the prophets should be called mystics but in this simpler sense of being drawn to God and wanting to live out of this thirst. The desire for God, however, is not weird or superhuman but a part of ordinary human experience. Some yield to it or are drawn to it more than others, to be sure, but part of God's action in the world is to reach out to each of us, pursuing us with love. Mystics are folk who live, responding to God's initiative, who pay attention, and who act in

---

3. Evelyn Underhill, *Life as Prayer* (Harrisburg, PA: Morehouse Publishing, 1991), 105, 107.

ways God directs. And, typically, they are people who are very engaged with life, not distant or withdrawn from it.

We tend to distance prophets in similar ways. Perhaps, as with saints, we admire their courage and persistent obedience. Or, as with mystics, we wonder at how they knew God's heart and understood God's message and action in their time. Even the runaway prophet, Jonah, failed to act at first because he knew God so well. He knew that God was so loving that, even against all the odds, if the worst people in the history of the world, the Ninevites, would repent, God would spare them. That made Jonah mad, and, in a grumpy obedience, he did the least he could to make that possible. While we recognize that the prophets were called to and empowered for specific tasks, they were not humans of an unapproachable category.

A fascinating thread running through the Bible suggests that, instead of simply admiring the prophets, the people of God individually and in community can share their identity and witness. A story about Moses gives us our first clue.

Moses complained so bitterly to God about the burden of leading Israel that he concluded, "If this is the way you are going to treat me, put me to death at once" (Numbers 11:15). God responded by promising to share some of the burden Moses bore with seventy of the elders of Israel by taking some of the spirit that was on him and putting it on them. When Moses had gathered the elders, God "took some of the spirit that was on [Moses] and put it on the seventy elders; and when the spirit rested on them, they prophesied" (11:25). As you might expect, two men invited didn't make the meeting, but the spirit rested on them anyway, back in the camp, and they prophesied. When people reported this to Moses, his assistant Joshua urged him, "My lord Moses, stop them!" To which Moses replied, "Are you jealous for my sake? Would that all the LORD's people were prophets, and that the LORD would put his spirit on them" (11:28–29). Though these elders did not continue to prophesy, Moses' hope that all of the people would be prophets is inviting.

After many years of prophets in Israel, many of whom we know about and many others we don't, this thread emerges again in the prophecy of Joel. After a period of restoration, Joel says,

God's promise is, "I will pour out my spirit on all flesh; your sons and daughters shall prophesy, your old men shall dream dreams, and your young men shall see visions. Even on the male and female slaves, in those days, I will pour out my spirit" (Joel 2:28–29).

In the life of the emerging Christian community, on the day of Pentecost, Peter quotes this prophecy of Joel to explain to the bewildered crowd how they were hearing unlearned Galileans speaking to them in their varied native languages. He says the exalted Jesus has poured out the Holy Spirit on the disciples, resulting in what they are seeing and hearing (Peter's speech in Acts 2:14–36). Peter later experiences and reports that while he was speaking (quite unexpectedly) to the Gentile audience at the centurion Cornelius's house, "the Holy Spirit fell upon all who heard the word," and they spoke in tongues and praised God (Acts 10:44–48; 11:15–18; 15:6–10).

Paul continues this thread of the people of God being prophets. In several places, Paul writes about the variety of empowered gifts that the Spirit gives to members of the community of faith, but in his letter to the church at

Corinth (1 Corinthians 14), he writes even more specifically about the gift of prophecy, explaining that it's even more important than the gift of tongues. "Those who prophesy," he writes, "speak to other people for their upbuilding and encouragement and consolation" (v. 3). And, he adds, even more than tongues, he would like all of them to prophesy (v. 5). He wants them to "be eager to prophesy" (v. 39). He adds instruction about when the community gathers together: "Let two or three prophets speak, and let the others weigh what is said" (v. 29). When things are done in good order, "you can all prophesy one by one, so that all may learn and all be encouraged" (v. 31). Clearly Paul saw prophecy as a widely available gift that serves to strengthen the body of Christ.

The Christian Scriptures mention several individuals who seem to have a heightened or specialized gift of prophecy that was recognized by the community. But they also honor the continuing thread of hoping that "all the Lord's people were prophets." They hold out the prospect that, individually and in community, we can all share the identity and the witness of the prophets, which is another reason to befriend and come alongside them. I know well that many folks resist taking for themselves the title "prophet" and shy away from regarding themselves as a prophet. I share that reluctance. But despite that, as the Spirit calls us out and empowers us, all of us can be visible signs and enduring witnesses to God among us. We can point to God's steady presence and to how the extravagant love of God pursues us. We can call people to join in the ongoing longing and work for renewal and healing restoration. We can invite folks to know God intimately and to embrace what God delights in—compassion, justice, and right living. We can join the prophets in being disturbing and helpful people for the love of God.

Captured by God

Surely the country singers in ancient Israel could belt out the tune:

> Mamas, don't let your babies
> grow up to be prophets.
> They'll scare you, they'll embarrass you,
> you'll think they've gone mad.

Now we don't have a diary or reports from Jeremiah's mom or Ezekiel's or Elijah's or bare-butt Isaiah's while he was walking around Jerusalem naked as a sign. But I bet they noticed, maybe blushed, and surely worried.

Mary, the mother of Jesus, noticed, too, when her son started wandering around Galilee, teaching and healing. She noticed that huge crowds followed him and pressed in on him so closely that he could hardly get a bite to eat. This report from the Gospel of Mark surprised me when I first really paid attention to it: "When his family heard what was happening, they came to take control of him. They were saying, 'He's out of his mind'" (Mark 3:21, CEB). Her prophet son gave her plenty of things to "ponder in her heart."

Since we have stories and messages from the prophets in the Hebrew Scriptures, we know that some folks cherished what they did and said. But many others resisted them. Kings and crowds scoffed, ignored, and threatened. So being a prophet was often discouraging and risky. Sometimes they had to run for their lives. Some weren't quick enough. Sometimes they moaned and complained. Jeremiah even said he was not going to speak in God's name anymore. But he couldn't stop. Why not? Why didn't the prophets just quit?

The prophets didn't exactly volunteer. The ones we read about in the Hebrew Scriptures didn't enroll at a prophet vo-tech thinking they would pursue a good, maybe even lucrative, career. Instead, God chose them to serve.

That's not to say that some folks didn't make good money at it. Some Israelites would consult "prophets" who would tell them what they wanted to hear or give them a favorable word from God if they paid the prophet enough money. Or maybe they could get a comfortable appointment as one of the royal prophets supported by the king or queen. Jeremiah and Ezekiel rebuked these message-for-hire folks, whom we still have around, as false prophets.

When the prophets tell us about God calling them, we can see common themes. (We see these, too, in other call stories.) First, God initiates the contact, perhaps in a burning bush, a vision or dream, or "a word of the Lord," and lays out the mission. Typically the prophet-to-be objects, "Who me? Do what? You definitely have the wrong person here." Moses objects that he doesn't talk well, for example, and Jeremiah that he's just a lad, perhaps in the sense of a nobody. God insists, though, that the candidate is not only the right choice but will also prevail with God's help. God often adds, "Don't be afraid. I'll be with you." I'm guessing that God doesn't need to tell the prophet what not to fear.

I don't think the prophets had much choice. Clearly Moses and Jeremiah didn't. Amos denied being a prophet, perhaps in some professional sense, but claimed that God told him, "Go, prophesy to my people Israel" (Amos 7:15). He explained further, "A lion has roared; who will not fear? The LORD God has spoken; who can but prophesy?" (3:8) People often present Isaiah as a bold volunteer when he says, "Here am I, send me," though in his vision he thought he was a dead man after encountering the glory and holiness of God. After being rescued, it's hard to imagine that when God asked, "Who will go for us?" that Isaiah would balk, "I'd just rather not." Nor do I imagine that Hosea was enthused about going to marry a "wife of whoredom." And we have the story of Jonah who tried to outrun a particular call, one in which God persisted.

The prophets we know about may not have volunteered, but they did respond in obedience. Why? Let me suggest that they were not just compelled but that they were also captured. In their encounters with God, they came to know God in ways that would not let them go.

Jeremiah gives us insight about what knowing God means in his famous oracle about boasting, or better, patting oneself on the back. He says:

> The LORD proclaims:
> the learned should not boast of their knowledge,
> nor warriors boast of their might,
> nor the rich boast of their wealth.
> No, those who boast should boast in this,
> that they understand and know me.
> I am the LORD who acts with kindness,
> justice, and righteousness in the world,
> and I delight in these things, declares the LORD.
> (Jeremiah 9:23–24 CEB)

Jeremiah isn't condemning boasting here as such. Instead, he's speaking about the reasons you might congratulate yourself, give yourself a pat on the back, or feel glad about. He warns against three of the most common boasts nations and individuals make: "I'm smart, I'm strong, I'm rich." Often with the subtext: "I'm better than you; don't mess with me."

But the more important point here is what we should be glad about instead: "Boast that

[you] understand and know me." The Jewish Publication Society aptly translates: "But only in this should one glory: In his earnest devotion to Me." The two key words point to both deep insight and a devoted relationship. As in many languages, the word "know" carries a wide variety of meanings that can range from superficial to intimate. Clearly here, the meaning is not just a knowing about God, a kind of abstract head-knowledge. It's knowing God by heart, a completely whole-hearted, relational knowing as the great command requires: "Love the Lord your God with all your heart, all your being, and all your strength" (Deuteronomy 6:5 the *Shema*). It's a kind of knowing that forms and guides and compels us.

The other word I find compelling here is the word "delight." It points to what God finds joy in, what God most cares about. Probably we all have relationships, whether kin or good friends, in which we learn what the other person likes and dislikes and in which we know almost instinctively what would bring joy to that person, even without having to ask. Perhaps you'll be traveling or shopping for a gift, and you'll say, "Karen would love these chocolates!" or "Fred would get a kick out of these argyle socks!" or maybe, "Chuck would hate this song! (or these argyle socks)," and you know you would be right. Because you know them.

What God delights in offers an enticing vision in itself. God longs for people to act justly, to show unrelenting mercy, and to live with each other, day to day, responsibly and generously. It's no accident that this sounds so much like Micah's description of what God requires: "Act justly, love kindness, and walk humbly with your God" (Micah 6:8). The first two words in Hebrew are the same, justice (*mishpat*) and kindness (*hesed*). Walking humbly with God comes very near the sense of knowing God.

Knowing God is something like knowing dear friends, except we discover that it goes well beyond just knowing what delights God. As we come to know God ever more fully, our hearts begin to be shaped more and more toward God's heart. We are steadily transformed until we share God's heart, until we ourselves delight in what God delights in.

In *The Prophets*, Abraham Heschel describes the pathos of God. Contrary to notions that God is distant, disengaged, unaffected, and unchanging (all remnants of gnostic teaching),

Heschel describes how the Bible insists that "God is concerned with the world."[4] God is present and actively pursuing what God delights in so that justice, compassion, and right living will prevail. God pays attention to what is going on and responds, whether with guidance or blessing, regret or rescue, warning or anger. God is near and is involved.

Heschel goes on to describe how the prophets have sympathy for God's pathos. They understand it and are molded by it. They speak and act out of what they know of God's presence, of God's heart. They are attuned to God's pathos. "The pathos of God is upon [the prophet]. It moves him. It breaks out in him like a storm in the soul, overwhelming his inner life, his thoughts, feelings, wishes, and hopes. It takes possession of his heart and mind, giving him the courage to act against the world."[5]

This way of knowing God surely is what moves the prophets beyond being compelled to being captured. How could you turn away? To what lesser presence? To what lesser love? To what lesser purposes and power? Little wonder

---

4 Heschel, II, 39.

5 ibid, 88.

that Jeremiah couldn't quit being present and speaking in the name of Yahweh. How could the way he knew God not be a "fire in his bones," something that he could neither renounce nor escape?

In his talk "Have You Ever Seen a Miracle?" Thomas Kelly describes people who have become "wholly God-enthralled." They have moved beyond devout practice or religious belief. They are folks who have had "moments of blinding vision" as they encounter God's holiness, splendor, and "the sheer beauty of [God's] persuading, all-embracing Love." They come to know God as "a living internal dynamic deep within us." And they come to live with the "royal-blindedness of Eternity." This comes both from God's persistent initiative and from the human willingness to yield to it and be transformed by it.[6] The prophets were God-enthralled people who were wholly gathered into God's active presence in the world. They saw it, collaborated in it, spoke and acted out of it. They were captured by God, and their faithfulness helps us see God more clearly ourselves.

---

6 Thomas Kelly, *The Eternal Promise*, 3 ed., (Richmond, IN: Friends United Press, 2016) 3 ed., 92–105.

Not everyone who knows and is captured by God in this way becomes a prophet, though their ordinary lives will witness to the vision of God they know. Many God-enthralled saints, whether famous, like Francis, Hildegaard, or Dorothy, or obscure, like Edith, Fred, Manuel, or Nancy, show the way and invite us to join them. And God persists in calling us all to know, understand, and share God's delight.

Compelling Vision

I have long loved the large framed print we have of Edward Hicks' "The Peaceable Kingdom of the Branch," one of the dozens of peaceable kingdoms that the Quaker sign painter created and that are still collected. It points us toward Isaiah 11, in which the prophet envisions a just, equitable rule where the lion lies with the lamb, the cow and bear graze together, a little child leads, and the earth is "full of the knowledge of the Lord just as the waters cover the sea" (Isaiah 11:1–9).

The prophets offer soaring images of the world God intends. Isaiah describes a reign of peace without limit, where justice and righteousness prevail (9:1–7). He also looks to a time when nations will stream to hear God's teaching and will beat their swords into plowshares, their spears into pruning tools (2:1–4). Amos calls on Israel to "let justice roll down like waters, and righteousness like an ever-flowing stream" (Amos 5:24). Israel's singers join in the vision, using words that often accompany each other in the prophets: "Faithful love and truth have met; righteousness and peace have kissed. Truth springs up from the ground; righteousness gazes down from heaven" (Psalm 85:10–11). Such grand words encourage us and inspire hope.

Yet such visions sometimes seem too lofty for us. As much as folks cherish these hopes, they may easily see them as too hard or too distant, as something they can't live or expect to see in their lifetimes. The prophets themselves make that seem sensible. They frequently call the Israelites out for failing to live into this vision. People lie and cheat, buy judges, plunder the poor, and find loopholes in agreements. Instead of creating tools for peace or beating swords into plowshares, they build bombs to protect their oil shares. They use both seed and labor to protect their power. The prophets weren't surprised, and neither are we.

Yet the prophets didn't give up. They urged people to live together in ways that made for peace (*shalom*). And they insisted that it isn't that complicated. That's the force of Micah telling folks that, despite their attempts at lavish offerings, they already knew what God requires: "do justice, love kindness, and walk humbly with your God" (6:8). A later prophet, Jesus, spoke simply, too: to love God and love your neighbor fulfills the Law and the Prophets (Matthew 7:12, 22:40).

When we examine some of the words the prophets use, we can get a clearer sense of how living well can be ordinary, even routine. Of the several words that frequently hang out together in the Prophets, let's look at four of the most common. The ones we've chosen here are righteousness (*tsedaqah*), justice (*mishpat*), love/kindness (*hesed*), and truth (*emunah*). I think of these as four shiny facets of the gem *shalom*. Instead of competing, they overlap and complement each other to build a community of peace.

In my experience, people often think of righteousness (*tsedaqah*) as an upgrade in someone's spirituality but also as a bit removed from ordinary life. But the prophets see righteousness as practical living. They point to daily ethical behavior, often with special attention to the poor and needy, the widow and the orphan, and to foreign resident ("strangers"). To be righteous is to live according to common norms, widely and readily accessible. I think they would agree with a local company that uses the slogan, "Doing the right thing matters." So be fair, be honest, add kindness and generosity.

When Job defends himself as a righteous man, he argues that he rescued the weak, shared his resources with the needy, looked after the widow and the orphan, "was eyes to the blind, feet to the lame," was fair in the market and in the court, and much more (Job 29:15ff., 31:16ff.).

In reviewing Job's defense, it is striking to see how often he refers to caring for vulnerable people. But this reflects the steady concern in the prophets (and in Israel's legal and wisdom literature) that folks should pay attention to the needs of people at risk. After all, these groups have the least resources, may be relatively hidden, and are the most readily mistreated. It's still easy to scam the elderly, to trap desperate people into debt, to mislead people who aren't fluent in local language and customs, to be closed off to the poor, or having noticed, to critique and ridicule them.

My friend Roger once pastored a church in a small town with premium real estate prices. One of the women in his congregation was suddenly widowed and, as is sometimes the case, was slow to understand and manage all her financial obligations. When Roger learned that the local bank was eagerly waiting to foreclose on her mortgage and sell her house, he hurried to the bank and challenged a bank officer, "What you're doing may be legal, but it's not right, and you're not going to do it." His attention and action spared her yet another loss.

So to be righteous, maybe a bit oversimply, is to do the right thing, steadily, habitually, daily, in our ordinary rounds. It is more often simple than grand or daring. After all, it's not that heroic to pay attention and be kind. In our time, shoppers and drivers might insist that righteousness includes the courtesy of recognizing that other shoppers and drivers actually exist. But it might also mean mowing somebody's lawn, helping with their groceries or kids, or taking a few minutes to chat. It might be helping to find housing or jobs for an immigrant family and being part of a supportive community. If you're running low on money in a restaurant, it might mean ordering a less expensive meal so you can still leave a generous tip. In the Jewish tradition, righteousness has come to include generosity or charity. Many Jewish homes keep *tzedaqah* boxes to collect contributions to give to the needy. Similarly, many folks offer help through organizations like Habitat for Humanity, Heifer International, Kiva, the Red Cross, and others.

Justice (*mishpat*) and righteousness often overlap each other. Sometimes the words are paired to mean "social justice." In Israel the idea of justice was rooted in their understanding of God's character, actions, and guidance. Certainly it included decisions taken by elders, courts, and kings, and it also included attention to the law. But it was more than that. Laws don't cover every circumstance, which is why we and they have case law, exploring how to act in specific instances. Sometimes laws are not just or are not justly applied. Of course, there are always legal scoundrels looking for loopholes and workarounds. And we know that people can undercut laws or, more broadly, justice in all sorts of ways. The prophet Amos called out merchants who used dishonest weights and mixed chaff in with wheat, and we have business inspectors today who still need to check weights, keep producers from injecting water into turkeys before they're frozen, and discourage builders from cheating on specs and materials.

But we can practice and pursue justice in simple and intentional ways. One easy way is to make honest deals. I once went with a friend who was buying a cord of wood. With the seller, he carefully counted the wood and reviewed the price, but I soon discovered he was not trying to sweeten the deal but only wanted to assure the seller that they had made a square deal. He made integrity show. A lot of folks think carefully about what goods and services they buy, eager to honor companies that treat people well. In a more enduring personal choice, I know a gifted lawyer who decided to spend his career as a public defender, advocating for those who often fail to get justice.

Beyond steady personal choices, we can find ways to collaborate with others in pursuing justice. It might be gathering in public witness about an issue or showing up at important public meetings such as school boards or city councils. One group organized to observe the local court over a three-month period every time it was in session. They wanted to see how users of the court were greeted, guided, and treated in the process. After their court-watching experience, they offered a list of suggestions to the court about how to improve its practices. The process was intentionally low-key and practical. Pursuing justice might require making calls or writing letters. It easily includes helping to support groups who work on justice issues. This can be pretty ordinary, though sometimes folks need to act in more daring and even dangerous ways. For some, it may even require civil disobedience done in good conscience.

The idea of love/kindness (*hesed*) may be the hardest to discuss since we don't have an adequate English word to express the meaning of the Hebrew word *hesed*. In Micah 6:8, translators use a variety of words to convey *hesed*: "love kindness," "love mercy," "love goodness," or, better than most, "embrace faithful love." But none of them convey the richness and depth of the word *hesed*. Of course, translation choices vary by context. A common translation is "steadfast love," but we see better the richness of *hesed* in how it's described. God's steadfast love lasts forever; I like Eugene Peterson's translation, God's love "never quits." It persists. It pursues, as in Psalm 23:6, "goodness and steadfast love shall pursue me all the days of my life."[7] God surrounds us with *hesed* and abounds with it. "For as the heavens are high above the earth, so great is his steadfast love" (Psalm 103:11). So words like kindness, goodness, and mercy point toward it but hardly capture it.

Remarkably, Micah says that God wants us to live embracing (actually, "loving") *hesed*. The character of God's love should guide our own. This challenges us to imagine how our love toward our neighbor can be generous and attentive, how it can persist and never give up, how it can be kind and compassionate, not just tolerant or polite. This love is not about feelings or about what one earns or deserves. Instead, it is a love of presence, desiring and working toward the best for the other. Such attentive care shapes us as loving persons who respond kindly where they are drawn.

---

7. Jewish Publication Society

A fourth word the prophets often use is truth (*emunah*). As a facet of *shalom*, it points toward reliability, dependability, of things being firmly established. Of course, the Bible often affirms that we can trust God as dependable. But part of the challenge in our ordinary living is that we should be reliable as well. People should be able to count on us. They should rely on our integrity. They should know that we're consistent, not capricious, that we'll do or say what's right, not merely convenient or whimsical or yielding to pressure.

We're not surprised, however, to know that some folks deliberately lie or mislead to reach their goals, often with great cynicism. Less ambitious, perhaps, many others are naive or careless about truth, recklessly passing along rumors and falsehoods. Such undercutting of truth in our common life creates chaos and confusion; it damages our life together. In contrast, we can develop daily habits that make us honest and reliable. We can live in ways that help build the community of peace.

We can act steadily to live into the compelling vision of what life together can be. This doesn't require perfection; we all know human weakness and failure. But this also refuses to push such visions into never-never land, assuming that people can't do what God asks of them. Instead, we can aspire to creating communities of *shalom* through ordinary action. We can develop daily habits of doing the right thing, of practicing and pursuing justice, of embracing *hesed* love, and of being honest and reliable people. The prophets challenge us to grand living even while they remind us that it really isn't that complicated.

Experienced Listeners

People have lots of practical questions about the prophets: How did they write? How have we gotten their messages? Perhaps more importantly: How did they know what to say? When? And to whom? How do they come to give a message from God?

It helps to know that we can't answer all of our questions. For some of them, the Bible itself doesn't give us enough information. And sound historical research shows us that we often don't know enough to give satisfying answers. Sometimes our best answers are educated guesses. Knowing our limits is better than embracing less careful assumptions and conjectures.

Today you don't have to be an office supply procurement specialist to have easy access to paper and notebooks; handy pens and pencils; folders and binder clips; newspapers, printed messages, and books; not to mention computers and printers; phones and internet service; email and text messages; or duplicating machines (printing presses, mimeographs, spirit duplicators, copiers—you can date yourself here). So it's hard to imagine that ancient Israelites and their neighbors had none of these. They did have writing tools. In Mesopotamia they wrote by creating wedge-shaped symbols (cuneiform) on wet clay tablets; in Egypt they wrote hieroglyphics on paper made from papyrus (and on lots of columns and walls); in Israel they used pen and ink on broken pottery or on leather crafted from animal skins. Some folks could read and write, but a high level of literacy was reserved for well-trained scribes, a privileged status in any of those cultures.

So it challenges our imaginations to wonder how the prophets wrote, at least physically. They don't give us any hints about a little nook stashed with writing tablets, pencils, and erasers. Or about legible manuscripts floating down from the sky. I'm puzzled. But I'm also intrigued by Jeremiah's report that he dictated twenty years worth of messages to the professional scribe Baruch, who wrote them on a scroll. And by him dictating it all again (and then some) after King Jehoiakim burned this first scroll column by column (Jeremiah 36). How did that happen? Did Jeremiah have an amazing memory (maybe some of his sermons were well-used and well-worn)? Or perhaps he lugged a big bag of potsherds he had scribbled sermon notes on? The best I can do here is tease and wonder and guess because I don't think we know.

Folks also wonder how these messages from the prophets got to us. A complete educated guess is long and complicated. We can be sure that the prophets weren't running vanity presses to churn out collections of oracles like "The Best of Amos" or "Hosea's Hottest Hits." And they weren't handing listeners copies of their talks when they got through. The short answer is that some people around the prophets valued and saved what the prophets said. They passed the prophetic words along, and eventually, the Israelite community as a whole embraced these messages as given by God to explain and guide their journey. These writings came to be treasured long before there was any vote on whether they should be on an official list.

The more important question, I think, is, "How did they know what to say?" The prophets' direct answer is most simply, "God spoke to me." They report that God communicated to them directly in a variety of ways, including words, dreams, and visions.

In our time, sometimes you'll see a printed T-shirt that reads, "I only do what the voices tell me," a reflection of modern cynicism about God speaking directly to folks. If Hebrew merchants had offered such shirts, Amos would have gladly worn one that said, "This wasn't my idea." His direct words were, "The LORD God has spoken; who can but prophesy?" (Amos 3:8; see also Amos 7:14–15). The prophets often recount such experiences. Beyond that, the Bible regularly shows, and the faithful through the ages witness, that God communicates with people directly. I won't argue against skepticism here but will simply note the abundant witness to God's speaking and will consider why we might think the prophets were reliable.

A key reason for receiving the prophets' messages is that they were experienced listeners. What they heard God telling them came in the context of their life with God, of their knowing and loving God. They knew directly that God delights in kindness (*hesed*), justice, and righteousness. They lived steadily in the covenant relationship that God had given Israel. The messages they heard did not seem remote or novel, though sometimes what God said caught them off guard.

When the lad, Samuel, heard someone calling to him in the night, eventually the priest, Eli, his mentor, told Samuel to respond, "Speak, Lord, your servant is listening" (1 Samuel 3:1–10). This sets the stage for his lifetime of prophetic faithfulness. Prophets come to know the voice, they listen, and they respond. Of course, prophets weren't the only ones who conversed with God. Lots of folks did (and do). But in their listening, God chose the prophets for their particular tasks.

In Samuel's stories, we see that God and Samuel sometimes have give-and-take about what Samuel should say and do, as when he went to Bethlehem to choose a new king from among Jesse's sons. We see that, too, in other prophets. Elijah and Jeremiah wanted to quit. Habakkuk objected that what God planned to do was outrageous, and he retreated to a fortress (a "watchtower") to see what would happen and listen for how God would respond.

But they were trustworthy; they spoke and acted in the ways that God told them to. They knew the difference between what God required them to say and what they might want to say. They offered guidance, correction, and hope as the times required, no matter whether their hearers received their words. Sometimes they urged people to change their ways just when folks thought everything was going well. For example, Jeremiah scolded false prophets for saying, "Everything is fine (Peace, peace)" when "there is/will be no peace" (Jeremiah 6:14). Similarly, he and others gave words of comfort and hope in times when the people were experiencing disaster. No doubt the prophets often felt they were paddling against the current. But they faithfully did what they were told, not speculating or venturing out on their own. The prophetic writings that we have witness to their trustworthiness.

The writings also tell stories of scoundrels, prophetic figures who were greedy and self-serving. Among other things, they would get good money for telling people what they wanted to hear. People in all times have rightly been suspicious of ambitious folks who embrace the label "prophet." But Israel's true prophets weren't serving to gain advantage or recognition. They weren't raising money to build mansions on lovely hillsides or to maintain a private stable of the finest DynoDonkeys to get them quickly and safely to their prophet gigs. Perhaps they remembered the cautionary (and funny) story of the "seer," Balaam, whose donkey saw better than he did (Numbers 22). Instead, they simply wanted to convey God's messages to the people Israel.

The occasions for the prophets to serve varied. Sometimes people consulted them to "seek the LORD," to get guidance about their problems or plans. For example, when King Ahab of Israel invited King Jehoshaphat of Judah to join in his battle plans to reclaim a border town from Aram (Syria), Jehoshaphat insisted, "Please, first inquire of the LORD." Ahab quickly rounded up four hundred prophets, but their unison promises of victory and dramatic choreography made

Jehoshaphat wary. So he objected, "Isn't there another prophet of the LORD through whom we can inquire?" So Ahab begrudgingly brought in Micaiah, whom he hated, "because he never prophesies anything good about me, only bad" (1 Kings 22). Not only kings, but others went to the prophets to help them know what God would have to say.

Sometimes the prophets were given specific messages or information to carry to others. I think some today might refer to these as "words of knowledge." For example, during a time when the king of Aram was plotting to invade Israel (these two fought a lot at that time), he would plot secretly where to station his troops to sneak up on Israel. But the king of Israel always seemed to know where to confront them. After his officers denied leaking the plans, they told Aram's king, "It's Elisha the Israelite prophet who tells Israel's king the words that you speak in the privacy of your bedroom" (2 Kings 6:12).

The prophet, Nathan, was told to confront David about having murdered Uriah, one of his most loyal soldiers, by exposing him in battle in order to take Bathsheba, his wife, into David's harem. David had tried to do this stealthily, so

Nathan's bold condemnation caught him off guard (2 Samuel 12).

A couple of centuries later, Sennacherib and the powerful Assyrian army surrounded Jerusalem, threatening to demolish it. In his annals, Sennacherib brags that he had Judah's King Hezekiah shut up "like a bird in a cage." Responding to the Assyrian's rants and threats, Hezekiah desperately prayed for deliverance. In response, the prophet Isaiah sent him specific messages, promising that Jerusalem would not suffer attack and that Sennacherib himself would return home and be overthrown (2 Kings 19).

Beyond being consulted or being sent with specific content to share, the prophets often spoke without invitation and (maybe) without people clamoring to hear what they had to say. In many instances, we can't describe where they spoke, but sometimes, based on their messages, we can imagine them in the marketplace or near the courts being held at the city gates or around folks involved in religious ritual and sacrifice. Beyond that, whether in palaces or at street corners, during festivals or in fields, we mostly don't know.

We may wonder still about why these particular messages in these times and places. Amos, for example, had often been in the marketplace and had seen merchants using false weights, cheating on their products, or taking advantage of vulnerable folk. And, because that's so clearly prohibited in Israelite law, he knew it was dead wrong. He could have railed against it at any time and probably called particular vendors by name. Jeremiah, from a priestly family, knew how religious hucksters were turning the holy courts of the temple into a den of thieves. He also saw the disconnect between splendid ritual and shoddy living. Isaiah knew how leaders warped words and how judges twisted justice. Without being given messages, they had plenty to say.

But they spoke as they were directed, when they were prompted. Sometimes, I'm sure, they knew they weren't to say anything. But at other times, they knew they had a message to bring, one that was clearly required, both timely and urgent. At this point we encounter the mystery of collaboration between God and those God calls to speak or pray or sing. We don't know how to easily describe the melding of what is crafted and what is given.

It helps, I think, to clarify what "word" means, as in the phrase, the "word of God." The Hebrew word *dabar* is very ordinary and is typically used to mean "word, thing, affair, something," subject to its particular context. So we might rightly think of the phrase "word of God" in a particular oracle as referring to the content, the message, the expression of what God is doing. But we need not read it "words of God" in the narrow sense that each word is spoken exactly by God, which leads mistakenly to seeing this process as dictation. Some find comfort in this narrower reading, but most interpreters recognize that various prophetic writers/speakers had different literary styles, vocabulary, and more. That is, they reveal individuality and craft.

This suggests how the phrase "mystery of collaboration" is useful. God is involved guiding a message (perhaps you would prefer "inspiring a message") and the writer is listening intently and crafting the message. It might flow, it might resist, and it might come in bits or all at once. And in the process, there may well be moments when the writer wonders, "Where did that word/phrase/image/tune come from?" And yet in the attention and struggle along with the surprises of it, a message to share comes clear.

I would like to know more; probably you would, too. Did they compose these speeches by hand? Did they, as oral poets do, compose them in their heads to remember and deliver? Did some of these oracles become stump speeches delivered here and there as needed? When, under the Spirit, they spoke these messages, were they sometimes surprised by what they heard themselves saying? (I had an English-speaking friend who was once stunned while leading a memorial service to hear himself, as he described it, "speaking in tongues in English.") With these and similar questions, I would love to have reliable answers. But this is one place that we should confidently say that we don't really know.

I'm convinced though that we can trust that the prophets were experienced listeners who learned what they were to do and say and who faithfully did it, whether they liked it or not. We can give thanks still for their faithfulness as their lives and words continue to guide us today.

Beyond Cranky

People often ask, "So who is a prophet today?" The variety in their answers reveals widely differing views of what the prophets said and how they said it. How we answer that question also suggests how well we understand the prophets in the Bible and how we can imagine prophetic ministry today.

People commonly caricature the prophets as loud and cranky. When reading prophetic texts aloud, readers often choose to shout, regardless of the meaning of text. And sometimes folks suggest that curmudgeonly, contrary folk among us are being prophetic. Both loud reading and thinking of contentious people as prophets can mislead us. Prophets often did criticize, of course, but they weren't just cranks. (And most cranks aren't prophets.) The prophets didn't just scold; they didn't just shout. We'll do well to take a more complete view of their message and ministry.

People in ministry sometimes wonder together about whether one can be both a pastor and a prophet. Pursuing an answer has lots of subtleties. I won't propose a conclusion here except to say that in many ways prophets did what pastors do; they cared for their people. As occasion required (and often out of urgency or crisis), they offered correction and guidance. They brought comfort. They held out hope. In some instances, the prophets prayed on behalf of others.

Messages of warning often include harsh language and shocking images. They can be disturbing to read. Even when we see poetic exaggeration at work here, still the experiences of destruction and deportation were as harsh as the words. Sharp warnings tried to jolt people to attention, to call them to turn back from the risky paths they were pursuing. The Hebrew word for repentance, *shub*, means to turn around, to change direction. This was the prophets' urgent call.

Generally such messages were pleas more than predictions. Through the prophets, God is pleading for the Israelites to return to their covenant relationship with God alone. Through Jeremiah, for example, God charges Israel with "two crimes: They have forsaken me, the spring of living water. And they have dug wells, broken wells that can't hold water" (Jeremiah 2:13). In this situation, the prophets remind people not only that they should not chase after or trust in other gods but also that they should live together steadily in what being God's people required. "Seek good and not evil, that you may live; and so the LORD, the God of heavenly forces, will be with you just as you have said" (Amos 5:14).

Often the prophetic message turns to teaching: serve the LORD alone, act justly, show compassion, take care of the vulnerable folk, and other familiar themes. So while they're rejecting phony but lavish religious celebration, the prophets teach, "Let justice roll down like waters, and righteousness like an ever-flowing stream," (Amos 5:24) and "do justice, embrace faithful love, and walk humbly with your God" (Micah 6:8).

Sometimes the prophets bring specific words of guidance about how the Israelites should act in the circumstances they face. For example, when Babylon has already conquered the Judeans and has installed a puppet king, Zedekiah, some prophets continued to urge rebellion. Jeremiah countered them with this message, "If you want to live, put your necks under the yoke of the king of Babylon and serve him and his people" (Jeremiah 27:12). King Zedekiah refuses to listen, and the country suffers even greater disaster. Later, Jeremiah sends a letter to Judeans who have been deported as exiles to Babylon. He advises, "Build houses and settle down; cultivate gardens and eat what they produce.... Increase in number there.... Promote the welfare of the city where I have sent you" (Jeremiah 27:5–7).

Often the prophets' messages bring stirring words of hope and restoration. Many of us know these themes still through the great choruses of Handel's oratorio "The Messiah": about a highway with valleys raised up and mountains made low, the glory of the Lord being revealed, comfort for the people, and the gentle care of the shepherd. Isaiah tells disheartened Israel that those who hope in the Lord will renew their strength, will fly up on wings like eagles (Isaiah 40). Jeremiah reminds exiles, "I know the plans I have in mind for you, declares the Lord; they are plans for peace, not disaster, to give you a future filled with hope" (Jeremiah 29:11). Through his story of an unlikely marriage, Hosea reminds Israel that God will pursue them in unending love to restore them.

Other messages of hope transcend their initial settings and continue to lift us. We still long for the Peaceable Kingdom and for the time when nations will beat swords into plowshares, tanks into tractors. We still want to share the courage of Habakkuk who, even in confusion, declared, "[Even when disaster strikes and the entire economy collapses], I will rejoice in the Lord. I will rejoice in the God of my deliverance. The Lord God is my strength. He will set my feet like the deer. He will let me walk upon the heights" (Habakkuk 3:18–19). We still lean into words of hope like, "Do not fear for I am with you. . . . I will strengthen you, I will help you" (Isaiah 41:10). These words come from the varied messages of the prophets, who loved their people and were not mere scolds.

The prophets not only had wide-ranging messages, but they also delivered their messages in a fascinating variety of ways. Of course they spoke, as we would expect, but they used varied speech forms. Often they used the language of courtrooms and indictment speeches when they were bringing Israel up on charges of unfaithfulness. When we see "woe" oracles, we know they were using the language of funerary practice as warning and lament. Sometimes we see them using satire or humor. The prophets gave striking reports of visions and of their dialogues with God. Nathan presented a story and legal case before David, who functioned as a high court, in calling him to account over the Bathsheba affair.

Isaiah introduces one of his prophecies by saying, "Let me sing for my loved one a love song for his vineyard" (Isaiah 5:1), and those of us who know the work of Woody Guthrie or Pete Seeger (and many others) surely would not be surprised to think that prophets might sing. I suspect Isaiah's hearers enjoyed it until he got to the killer refrain. Of course, many of the prophetic oracles we have are written in poetry, so it's not hard to imagine that some of them may have been sung.

The prophets also used symbolic actions to convey their messages, sometimes on single occasions and others in adopting a lifestyle of witness. God told Jeremiah, for example, never to marry and have children since the times ahead would be disastrous. He was also to avoid joining in funerals or feasts, again as a warning of trouble to come (Jeremiah 16). Hosea was told to "go marry a prostitute" (Hosea 1:2), a continuing witness to Israel's unfaithfulness and God's pursuing love. People debate whether this was an action or a parable, but in either case, it is a powerful symbol. God told Ezekiel to lie on his side in the street in Jerusalem next to a model of the city under siege for 430 days. He not only was doing street theater but also became a street fixture! We know examples of lifestyle witness over many years, so prophets using it should not surprise us.

Single actions could be vivid and powerful. Jeremiah, for example, bought a new linen "undergarment" (clearer to modern readers than "loincloth," and more polite than "BVDs") and went to bury it under a rock at a riverbank. He later went to recover it after it "was ruined and good for nothing" (Jeremiah 13). He also wore an ox yoke and smashed pottery to give a clear message. Ezekiel gave himself a haircut with a sword and took actions with the hair he had cut (Ezekiel 5). He also enacted ("make sure people are watching!") going into exile by packing refugee baggage and digging a hole in a wall to escape (Ezekiel 12). And Isaiah going naked and barefoot in Jerusalem for three years surely caught people's attention (Isaiah 20).

The words and actions of the prophets, in all their variety, are both vivid and memorable. Some of the words are so vivid, in fact, that they don't get read aloud during public worship or in children's classrooms (parents don't want to explain). The words' intensity and high exaggeration leave their mark, as they intend, as do the bold actions.

Paying close attention to the varied words and actions can make us better readers. We can read more imaginatively, not routinely assuming a single approach. Poets choose words carefully; we can ponder their choice. We can visualize both words and actions. And, stretching a bit to overcome cross-cultural barriers, we might even try to understand what it cost the prophets to speak or act in those ways.

If, as I've suggested, God continues to prompt people to give a prophetic witness, these examples may guide us. I expect that such messages will cover the full range of warning, teaching, guidance, comfort, and hope, whether to individuals or to groups. Perhaps this witness will be vivid and memorable, too. However, whatever shape it takes, it will grow from the mystery of divine-human collaboration. Being prompted (called, nudged, compelled) will lead to particular occasions, fresh forms, and timely words. It should not just imitate witness from other times. For example, historically, some folks have imitated Isaiah and have gone "naked as a sign," with mixed results. Mimicking the faithfulness of others usually doesn't meet the moment.

Speaking and acting in our contemporary settings may require new forms. Surely songs and poetry and art will continue to bring a strong message. New actions such as pouring blood over or hammering on nuclear warheads have had a fresh power, though this never would have occurred to Jeremiah. We can expect that as we respond to leadings, God will stir up in us apt words to evoke compassion, to lead to justice, to give comfort and hope.

Seeing the variety of messages and methods the prophets used can sharpen our understanding of who they were. It can focus our sense of what a prophetic message might look like today and of who might deliver it. And it can remind us that God chooses surprising people in unexpected times and places.

Scripture Index

Numbers
11:15 27
11:25 27
11:28–29 27
22 59

Deuteronomy
6:5 36

1 Samuel
3:1–10 57

2 Samuel
12 61

1 Kings
22 60

2 Kings
6:12 60
19 61

Job
29:15 44
31:16 44

Psalm
23:6 49
85:10–11 42
103:11 49

Isaiah
2:1–4 42
5:1 70
9:1–7 42
11 41
11:1–9 41
20 72
40 69
41:10 69

Jeremiah

2:13	67
6:14	58
9:23–24	35
13	72
16	71
27:5–7	68
27:12	68
29:11	69
36	55

Ezekiel

5	72
12	72

Hosea

1:2	71
6:6	22

Joel

2:28–29	28

Amos

3:8	34, 56
5:14	67
5:24	22, 67
7:14–15	56
7:15	34

Micah

6:8	22, 37, 43, 48, 68

Habakkuk

3:18–19	69

Matthew

7:12	43
22:40	43

Mark

3:21	32

Acts

2:14–36	28
10:44–48	28
11:15–18	28
15:6–10	28

1 Corinthians

14	29

www.ingramcontent.com/pod-product-compliance
Lightning Source LLC
Chambersburg PA
CBHW021320110426
42743CB00050B/3432